ide Annual

My favourite animal

Draw or stick a picture of your favourite animal here.

All about Rainbows

My Rainbow unit is ....

We meet on ....

My Rainbow Guider is called ....

Turn the page to see what's inside your 1999 Rainbow Guide Annual!

My Rainbow Guide Promise

I will do my best to love my God and to be kind and helpful.

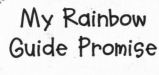

 1999

It's full of fun!

Inside your 1999

Goody Bag researched by Victoria Wheater;
A Very Special Birthday written by Susan Allan;
Guinea-pigs, Chinese New Year, Teddy Bears'
Picnic, Make Your Body Work, Summertime and
Rainbow Beads researched and written by John
Malam; T-Shirt Fun and Crispy Choccy Surprise
researched and written by Hilary Edwards-Malam.

Special thanks to: RSPCA (Guinea-pigs); Rainbow
Guides from 4th Mill Hill Rainbow Guide Unit
(Body Talk); Rainbow Guides from 1st London
Colney Rainbow Guide Unit (Make Your Body
Work and On the Milky Way); Lee Woodruff at
The Pinnacle, St Albans (Make Your Body Work);
Stella Lee and all the staff of Bowmans Open Farm
(On the Milky Way); Raleigh Industries Limited
(Win a Mountain Bike).

1999 Rainbow Guide Annual
© The Guide Association 1998

Front cover photography by Diana Aynaci;
Guinea-pigs, Work out the Wildlife and Chinese
New Year photography © RSPCA Photolibrary
and TRIP Photographic Library; Beetle photograph
(Colour Crazy) © TRIP/J Ringland; Friesian cow
photographs (On the Milky Way) © RSPCA/Colin
Seddon and RSPCA/Tim Sambrook; Win A
Mountain Bike photography © Raleigh Industries
Limited; 'The Alien' by Julie Holder; from A Third
Poetry Book compiled by John Foster, published by
O.U.P. © Julie Holder; 'Big Sister and Little Sister' by
Charlotte Zolotow reprinted by permission of
William Heinemann (a division of Reed
International Books Ltd) © Charlotte Zolotow.

Published by The Guide Association
17–19 Buckingham Palace Road
London SW1W 0PT
E-mail: chq@guides.org.uk
Web site: http://www.guides.org.uk

An official publication of The Guide Association
(incorporated by Royal Charter)
Registered charity number 306016
ISBN 0 85260 149 2
The Guide Association Trading Service
ordering code 60046

Rainbow Guide Adviser: Susan Butler
Project Editor: Clare Jefferis
Publications Manager: Anne Moffat
Studio: Gillian Webb, Joanna Harkness, David Jones
Caroline Marklew, Catherine Summers.
Colour repro by Graphic Facilities.
Printed and bound in Belgium by Proost NV.

Rainbow Annual

Rainbow Guides enjoy a balanced programme of activities covering eight points. These badges appear on pages to show how activities fit in with the Rainbow programme.

Safety is always an issue when trying any activity. Many of the activities within this Annual require adult help or supervision.

Goody Bag

You need

binca (12cm x 25cm)

coloured wool
darning needle

2 paper clips

badge   glue

sequins, buttons, bows

Keep your hair slides, pony-tail scrunchies and other bits and pieces in this bag.

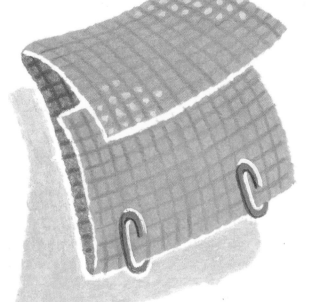

1 Fold the binca into three parts as shown. Use paper clips to hold the bottom flap in place.

2 Thread the needle. Tie a knot at the end of the wool. Sew along each side of the binca.

3 Fold the top flap over. Stick or sew on sequins, buttons and bows. Put a piece of paper behind the flap when gluing!

PVA GLUE

4 Pin your favourite badge on the front. This will keep your bag closed!

You can buy binca from most fabric and craft shops.

Pictures by Frances Lloyd

A Very Spec

1 It was Mrs Smith's special birthday. The Rainbows were planning a surprise party.

2 They decorated a cake. "Mmm, I can't wait to have some!" said Sufia.

3 "Let's make a card," said Nicola. "What about a present?" asked Jade.

4 The girls bought a plant for their friend. "That's 99p please," said the shopkeeper.

Pictures by Claire Spooner

5 The Rainbows got on the bus. They were careful not to drop their goodies.

6 "Happy Birthday!" the Rainbows cried when Mrs Smith opened her door.

7 At the party they played lots of games. Then Mrs Smith blew out her candles.

8 "I've had a lovely time," said Mrs Smith. "This has been the best birthday ever!"

Can you guess how old Mrs Smith is?

Use a mirror to find some surprises on this page.

Seeing things
When you look in a mirror you see yourself. This is called a **reflection**.

Ask a friend to be your reflection. Stand looking at each other. Get your friend to copy your movements. Afterwards swap over.

Secret writing
Hold your mirror on the red line. Read the message. What does it say?

Rainbows have fun

Pictures by Paula Martyr

agic

Funny mirrors

Mirrors that are curved
make you look different.
Look into a shiny spoon.
What do you see?

Turn the spoon over.
Look at yourself again.
Do you look different?

Mirror tricks

See what happens to these
pictures with your mirror.

1 Can you
find a
butterfly?

2 Can you make
two Rainbows?
Bring them
close together?
Make them
far apart?

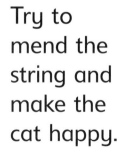

3 Try to
mend the
string and
make the
cat happy.

How well
did you do?
Answers
page 60.

11

Funny Faces

Give these biscuits a face lift! They are great to eat on Red Nose Day.

Ingredients

digestive biscuits

glacé cherries

icing sugar

water

sweets

red food colouring

You need

2 mixing bowls

palette knife

teaspoon

knife

icing sugar

1 Mix the icing sugar and water to make a stiff paste.

Pictures by Sonia Canals

2 Take half the paste. Mix in a few drops of food colouring until pink.

3 Spread a teaspoon of icing over the biscuit.

4 Cut a cherry in half. Stick on to the icing to make a nose.

Ask a grown-up to help you slice!

5 Add 2 smarties for eyes. Use liquorice laces for mouth and hair.

Red Nose Day is on 12 March 1999.

Guinea-

Find out about these cute creatures. They also make great pets!

In the wild

Guinea-pigs come from South America where they live in burrows. They have a chunky body with a short tail which you cannot see.

RSPCA/E A JANES

My pet guinea-pig

Guinea-pigs need a warm hutch to live in and a place to run around. Give them fresh water and food every day.

pigs

Furry friends

Some guinea-pigs have short, smooth fur. Others are tufty. Some even have hair that grows to the ground! They can be white, black, brown, grey, orange or a mix of colours.

RSPCA/JUDYTH PLATT

A guinea-pig lives for 4–6 years.

TRIP/M THORNTON

Sharp teeth

Guinea-pigs have sharp front teeth that never stop growing. To keep them short they must bite on something hard to wear them down.

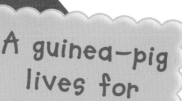

RSPCA/ANGELA HAMPTON

RSPCA/KEN MCKAY

Pet talk

David Grant, RSPCA vet and star of *Animal Hospital*, gives his pet care tips.

★ Be gentle. Pick up your guinea-pig with both hands.

★ Talk to your guinea-pig. Stroke it every day.

★ Guinea-pigs need vitamin C. Give your pet hay, fruit and vegetables to eat.

Starfish spot
There are lots of orange starfish hiding in this picture. How many can you spot? How many legs does each starfish have?

Go dotty
Join the dots. Which sea creature can you find?

1

2

3

4

5

Picture by Jill Newton

T-Shirt Fun

You need

plain T-shirt

fabric crayons

pencil

sheet of drawing paper

a pad of paper (the same size as the drawing paper)

iron and ironing board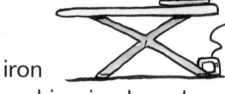

Wear your own work of art. No-one will have a T-shirt like it!

1 Draw a picture on the piece of paper. Colour it in using the fabric crayons.

! Never use an iron by yourself.

2 Put the pad of paper inside the T-shirt.

Pictures by Caroline Jayne Church

3 Carefully lay your drawing face down on the T-shirt.

4 Ask a grown-up to iron over the paper. Use a hot, dry iron.

A press and lift movement is better than a to and fro movement.

5 Lift the paper. Your picture is now on the T-shirt!

Do not use any letters or words. They will come out back to front on your T-shirt.

The Alien

The alien
Was as round as the moon.
Five legs he had
And his ears played a tune.
His hair was pink
And his knees were green,
He was the funniest thing I'd seen
As he danced in the door
Of his strange spacecraft,
He looked at me –
And laughed and laughed!

Picture by David Le Jars

Body

We don't have to say anything to tell someone how we feel. Our body speaks for us.

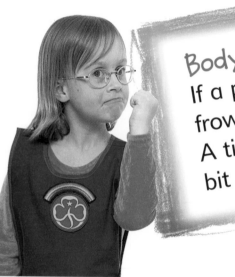

Body movements

If a person is angry she may frown and screw up her face. A tired girl might move a bit slower and yawn.

angry

tired

How do these girls feel?

Photographs by Diana Aynaci

Things to try

Talk

Mime game
Some people act out stories without talking. This is called mime.

1 Pick a book, film, song or TV programme to mime.

4 Now mime the first word.

2 Mime what you have picked. Is it a song or a book?

5 Mime the second word.

3 How many words are there?

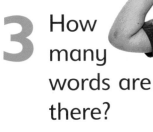

6 Mime the third word.

Can you guess what it is?

Now play this with a friend. Remember mime one word at a time.
If there are any words you get stuck with, move on to the next word.

How well did you do? Answers page 60.

Sunny Side

A yummy breakfast for a sunny day.

Ingredients

 a thick slice of bread

 an egg

 margarine or butter

You need

 chopping board

 greased baking tray

 biscuit cutter

 knife

 saucer

Pre-heat the oven to gas mark 6/200°C/400°F.

Ask a grown-up to help!

1 Butter one side of the bread.

24

Pictures by Caroline Jayne Church

Up

2 Cut a shape in the middle of the bread. Put both bits on to a greased baking tray.

3 Break the egg into a saucer. Carefully slide it into the hole in the bread.

4 Bake in the oven for 7 minutes. Then tuck in!

Turn the page to find out more about the sun.

Summerti

Summer is the warmest, brightest season of the year.

Hot spot
The Sun is really a huge star. It sends light and heat to Earth so that plants, animals and humans can live. You must never look straight at the Sun.

Summer creatures
Bees and butterflies fly from flower to flower to feed. Swallows can also be seen. Other birds and animals are out and about too, feeding and playing.

Explore Discover

Picture by Jacqueline East

Sticky storms

When the weather gets hot and sticky, there are sometimes exciting storms with thunder and lightning.

Dark day

If the sun hides behind the moon it gets very dark. This is called an eclipse and doesn't happen very often. There will be one on 11 August 1999.

Pretty picture

Fields are filled with colourful flowers such as poppies, buttercups, daisies and honeysuckle.

Work out

Look at these pictures. Can you find a giraffe, ladybird, frog, goldfish, zebra, hedgehog, butterfly and flamingo?

1

RSPCA/KLAUS-PETER WOLF

2

RSPCA/BIRGIT KOCH

3

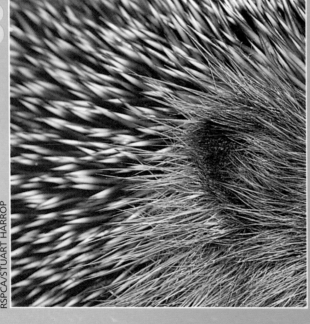

RSPCA/STUART HARROP

4

RSPCA/DAVE BEVAN

the Wildlife

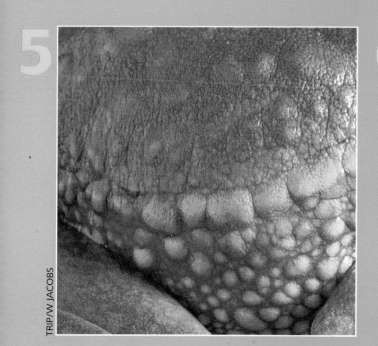

5

TRIP/W JACOBS

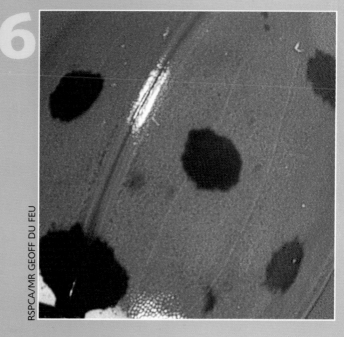

6

RSPCA/MR GEOFF DU FEU

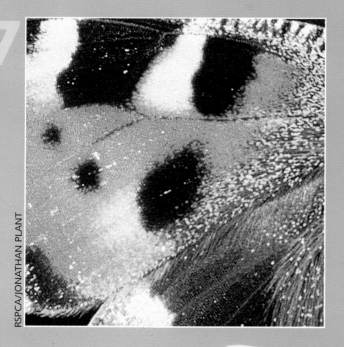

7

RSPCA/JONATHAN PLANT

8

RSPCA/BIRGIT KOCH

How well did you do?
Answers page 60.

A Year to

Make this treasure box all about you!
Hide it away for a year. See how you change.

You need

large empty box

Make it special
Paint it your favourite colour. Cover it with pictures of your favourite animals.

Inside your box
Put in lots of things about yourself. Here are some ideas to help you.

Draw yourself
Lie on a big piece of paper. Ask a friend to draw round you. Paint yourself in your best clothes. Write your age on the back. Roll it up.

Your favourite things
A photo of your pet. A poster of your number 1 pop group.

Picture by Caroline Jayne Church

Make and do
Remember

Rainbow fun
Draw what you like doing at Rainbows. What colour tabard do you wear?

School stuff
Draw your teacher and the things you like about school.

Ask a grown-up to put it somewhere safe. Remember no peeking!

The year 2000
Open your box. Do you look different now? Have you grown?

Teddy Bears'

The  were excited. They had been asked by

their leader Miss , who they called

to bring teddies to the Rainbow meeting. "This is my

niece, Karen," said . "She comes from South

Africa." The packed their 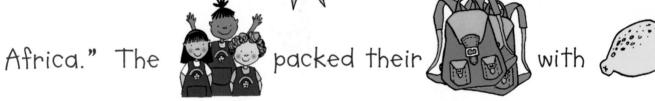 with

squash, ,  and . "Don't forget

your ," said their Unit Helper Miss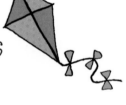

who they called . The  walked to the

 with  and . They sat on a

 and started their picnic. Karen told

Pictures by Alison Carney

them about South Africa. "Did you know there are no

there? But there are 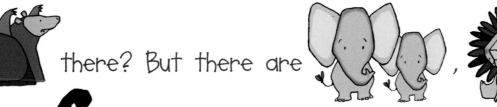,

and ," she said. Rachel wanted to know about

Karen's . "It's got a  on it because in

South Africa are called Teddies," said Karen.

Suddenly there was a roaring noise from behind a

. "I hope that wasn't a !" said Karen.

"It's only pretending to be one!" said .

"There are no  here, either." "Only our

bears!" said Rachel. They all laughed.

Make Your

Enjoy a fun work out with these simple exercises.

Listening Moving

Spin the hoop

1 Stand up straight with your feet a little bit apart. Hold the hoop around your waist.

2 Gently move your hips and bottom in a circle movement.

Bend your knees a little.

3 Now let go of the hoop! Swing it around your waist keeping your hips and bottom moving. How long can you keep the hoop going?

Forward roll

1 Crouch down. Lift your heels off the ground. Hold your arms out in front to stop yourself from wobbling.

34

Body Work

Standing on one leg

1 Stand on one leg. Count to 10 slowly. Try not to wobble or fall over.

2 Now hold your leg out to the side. Count to 10 again. Did you wobble?

3 Try doing the same again standing on your other leg.

2 Put your palms on the floor. Tuck your head in between your hands, close to your knees.

3 Push forward with your feet and gently roll over.

4 As you roll, push down with your hands so you roll back on to your feet.

Photographs by Diana Aynaci

Fruit Squ

Cool down with this summer treat.

Ingredients

fruit squash  water

You need

clean, empty yoghurt pot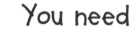

food wrap

lolly stick

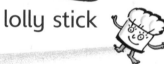

1 Half-fill a clean yoghurt pot with fruit squash.

2 Fill the rest of the pot almost to the top with water.

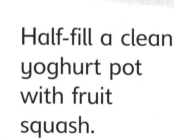

Pictures by Sonia Canals

ash Lolly

3 Cover the top with food wrap. Poke a lolly stick through the middle of the wrap.

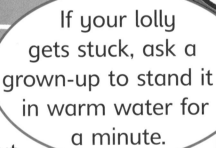

4 Put the pot in the freezer. Leave until frozen.

If your lolly gets stuck, ask a grown-up to stand it in warm water for a minute.

5 Pop it out of the pot and enjoy your lolly!

Mmm yummy!

Try these cool flavours

★ For a stripy lolly, freeze different flavour squashes, one layer at a time.

★ Milk mixed with a few drops of vanilla makes an ice-cream treat!

Chinese New

New Year does not have to start on 1 January. This year the Chinese celebrate New Year on February 16.

Lucky money
Children are given red envelopes filled with money. This is for good luck and wealth.

TRIP/J MOSCROP

TRIP/H ROGERS

TRIP/A TOVY

Fun and dance
Families let off fireworks and bang drums. The noise scares bad luck away. People dance through the streets dressed up as lions and dragons.

Festive food
Families enjoy a special meal without any meat. This is because each Chinese year has an animal name.

TRIP/TRIP

TRIP/TRIP

fun game with

4

5

Wear odd socks. Go back to start.

6

7

You need
a dice
a counter each

Eat a healthy breakfast. Have another go.

1

Brush your teeth. Move 1.

31

32

Forget to brush your teeth. Go back 3.

Start

33

Finish

35

How to play

★ The player who throws the highest number starts.

34

Remember to say goodnight. Have another go.

★ The first player to finish the game and go to bed is the winner.

Playground pu
See-saw, slide, swing, sandpit
sun, squirrel, skipping rope
skates, sandwiches, satchel
and spider.

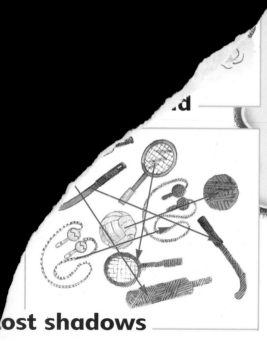

ost shadows

Arabian nights

Colour Crazy
pages 48–49
Colour mix up
1. Green leaves and red
berries on holly.
2. Black and white penguin.
3. Brown chocolate.
4. Yellow bananas, orange
oranges, yellow pineapple
green apple and red
cherries.

Around the World
pages 54–55
Noodle muddle
A is eating the noodles
from the bowl.

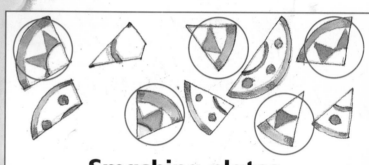

Smashing plates

Year

Seeing red
People wear red clothes.
Red is the colour of joy
and happiness.

TRIP/A TOVY

Year of the Rabbit
The Chinese
name each
year after
an animal.
1999 is the
year of the Rabbit.
  The Chinese
believe that rabbits
are kind and work
hard. They think that
people born in this
year are like this too.

RSPCA/COLIN CARVER

When were you born?
★1992 Year of the monkey
  You are friendly.

★1993 Year of the rooster
  You are brave.

★1994 Year of the dog
  You can be trusted.

RSPCA/E A JANES

RSPCA/E A JANES

RSPCA/KEN McKAY

Be a Sp[o...]

Splashing around
Look at the pictures below. There are 6 differences between them. How many can you see? Circle each one you find.

Lost shadows
These sporty objects have lost their shadows. Can you match them up?

rt!

How well did you do?
Answers page 60.

Pictures by Paula Martyr

Rainbow Beads

Make this pretty necklace for yourself or a friend.

Salt dough

You need

mixing bowl

 spoon

plastic bag

Ingredients

200ml water

 300g flour

300g salt

 30ml vegetable oil

Pre-heat the oven to gas mark ½/120°C/250°F.

1 Mix the flour and salt. Stir in the water a little at a time.

2 Mix in the vegetable oil. Knead on a floured worktop until it is firm.

3 Put in a plastic bag. Place in fridge for 30 minutes.

Pictures by Sonia Canals

4 Take pieces of mixture about the size of ping-pong balls. Shape into beads.

Necklace

You need

baking tray lined with greaseproof paper

PVA glue

paintbrush

string or ribbon

acrylic paints

5 Make a hole through the middle of each bead.

6 Place on a baking tray. Bake for 4 hours. Leave to cool.

Ask a grown-up to help!

7 Paint them bright colours and leave to dry. Cover with PVA glue. Leave overnight.

Try making a fridge magnet or badge.

8 Thread the beads on to string or ribbon.

Big Sister and

Once there was a big sister and a little sister. The big sister always took care. Even when she was skipping, she took care that her little sister stayed on the path. When she rode her bicycle, she gave her little sister a ride. When she was walking to school, she took the little sister's hand and helped her across the road. When they were playing in the fields, she made sure little sister didn't get lost.

When they were sewing, she made sure little sister's needle was threaded and that little sister held the scissors the right way. Big sister took care of everything, and little sister thought there was nothing big sister couldn't do. Little sister would sometimes cry, but big sister always made her stop. First she'd put her arm around her, then she'd hold out her handkerchief and say, "Here, blow."

Pictures by Jacqueline East

Little Sister

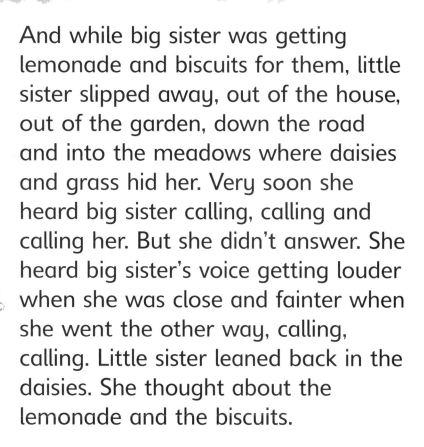

Big sister knew everything.
"Don't do it like that," she'd say.
"Do it this way."
And the little sister did. Nothing
could bother big sister. She knew
too much. But one day little sister
wanted to be alone. She was tired
of big sister saying,
"Sit here."
"Go there."
"Do it this way."
"Come along."

And while big sister was getting
lemonade and biscuits for them, little
sister slipped away, out of the house,
out of the garden, down the road
and into the meadows where daisies
and grass hid her. Very soon she
heard big sister calling, calling and
calling her. But she didn't answer. She
heard big sister's voice getting louder
when she was close and fainter when
she went the other way, calling,
calling. Little sister leaned back in the
daisies. She thought about the
lemonade and the biscuits.

45

She thought about the book big sister had promised to read to her. She thought about big sister saying,
"Sit here."
"Go there."
"Do it this way."
"Come along."

No one told little sister anything now. The daisies bent back and forth in the sun. A big bee bumbled by. The weeds scratched her bare legs. But she didn't move.

She heard her big sister's voice coming back. It came closer and closer and closer. And suddenly big sister was so near, little sister could have touched her.

Big sister sat down in the daisies. She stopped calling. And she began to cry. She cried and cried just the way little sister often did. When the little sister cried, the big one comforted her. But there was no one to put an arm around big sister. No one took out a handkerchief and said, "Here, blow." Big sister just sat there crying all alone.

Little sister stood up, but big sister didn't even see her, she was crying so much. Little sister went over and put her arm around big sister. She took out her handkerchief and said kindly, "Here, blow."
Big sister did. Then the little sister hugged her.
"Where have you been?" big sister asked.
"Never mind," said little sister. "Let's go home and have some lemonade."

And from that day on little sister and big sister both took care of each other because little sister had learned from big sister and now they both knew how.

Reprinted by permission of William Heinemann (a division of Reed International Books Ltd) © 1966 by Charlotte Zolotow.

Colour Crazy

The world is a colourful place. What would it be like in black and white?

Colour mix up

Some things we know by their colour. Post boxes are red, grass is green. Look at the 4 objects on this page. They are the wrong colours. What colours should they really be?

1

2

3

4

Which meal would you rather eat?

A

B

How well did you do?
Answers page 60.

Pictures by Jill Newton

Paint a rainbow

Did you know you can paint a rainbow using just 3 colours?

Red, yellow and blue are called primary colours.

Mix yellow and a little red to get orange.

Now add a little more red. Has the colour changed?

Hidden colour

Some animals use colour to help them hide. Can you find the beetle in this picture?

TRIP/J RINGLAND

Draw a rainbow shape on white paper. Use the numbers below to help you paint the colours in the right place.

1 Paint

2 Mix   and   to get

3 Paint

4 Mix   and   to get

5 Paint

6 Mix   and   to get

7 Mix   and   to get

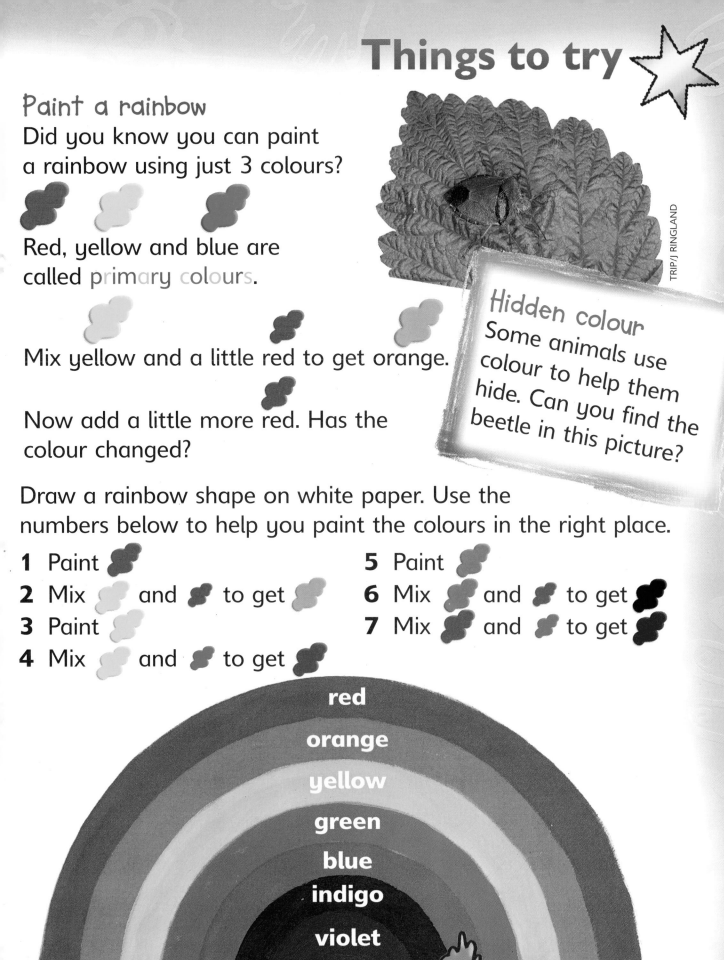

red

orange

yellow

green

blue

indigo

violet

1 2 3 4 5 6 7

Crispy Cho

Try this ice-cream treat.
It's so easy to make!

Ingredients

 slices of banana

2 dessertspoons of honey

75g puffed rice cereal

 glacé cherries

1 teaspoon of water

1 teaspoon of cocoa

ice-cream

You need

ice-cream scoop

small mixing bowl

2 glasses

1 Mix the honey, cocoa and water together to make the chocolate sauce.

Pictures by Tom Clayton

cy Surprise

2 Pop a cherry in each glass. Add 2 scoops of ice-cream and some banana.

Ask a grown-up to help you slice.

3 Put in 2 dessertspoons of cereal and a teaspoon of chocolate sauce.

4 Add more layers until you reach the top of the glasses.

More ice-cream is eaten in America than anywhere else in the world!

On the Mil

Do you know where milk comes from? Find out with Hannah, Lauren and Chloe down on the farm.

1 Meet the cows

The Rainbows arrive at the farm and meet Stella. She works at the farm and shows them around.

These cows are called Friesians. They make the most milk. They have to eat lots of grass.

2 The Learning Centre

The Rainbows find out that cows have 4 stomachs. No wonder they can eat so much grass!

3 Milking time

Stella shows Chloe the milking cups. The farmer fits the cups on to the cow's udder. The milk is then sucked into a big vat.

Before drinking, the milk is heat-treated. This kills any germs in the milk.

4 Ready to drink

Mmm yummy.

At last it's ready! Chloe gets to taste the milk first.

Moo!

Full up with milk, it's time to go home. The Rainbows say goodbye to Stella and Gypsy!

Thanks to Bowmans Open Farm for their help with this feature.

Photographs by Diana Aynaci

Elephant watch
You can see lots of elephants in Africa. Test your drawing skillls and copy this elephant picture in the grid.

Noodle muddle
In China they love to eat noodles. Can you work out who is eating the noodles from the bowl?

Pictures by Paula Martyr

World

Arabian nights
These two Rainbows and their Guider are in Egypt. There are 6 mistakes in this picture. Can you spot all of them?

Smashing plates
When the Greeks celebrate they sometimes smash plates on the floor. Match up the broken pieces to make two plates.

How well did you do? Answers page 60.

Apple Tr

Plant a tree for the next century. Watch it grow.

You need

clean plant pot and saucer

food wrap

potting compost or garden soil

small stones

apple pips

1 Soak some apple pips in water. Leave overnight. Put some stones in a pot.

2 Fill almost to the top with soil. Pop the pips on top. Cover with soil and water well.

Pictures by Jill Newton

3 Cover with food wrap. Keep in a warm, dark place until the pips sprout.

4 Take off the food wrap. Move to a sunny window-sill.

5 As it grows, move to a bigger pot. Later on plant your tree in the garden.

Don't forget to water your plant!

How would you like to ride off on your very own mountain bike? Enter our competition and you can!

This Raleigh Max bike is a must for any action girl! It has a bright orange frame so you are sure to be seen, an amazing 15 gears and chunky tyres. Riding a bike can be thirsty work so it comes with a matching water bottle too!

ntain Bike

Great prizes up for grabs!

Riding rules

★ Always wear a safety helmet when riding your bike.

★ Do not ride your bike out on your own. Always ask a grown-up to go with you.

★ Never ride on the road.

RALEIGH
NOTTINGHAM ENGLAND

For any information about Raleigh bikes call the Raleigh Brochure line on 0115 9163519.

How to enter

We have two of these brilliant bikes to give away. To win one all you have to do is:

1 Design a colourful outfit to wear on your bike. You must include a safety helmet with your outfit.

2 Write on the back of your drawing:

★ Your name, address and age.

★ How tall you are. We need to know this so we can order the right size bike.

★ Your favourite three things in this Rainbow Guide Annual.

Be careful your writing doesn't show through and ruin your drawing!

3 Send your entry in an envelope to:

Win a Bike Competition
1999 Rainbow Guide Annual
The Guide Association
17-19 Buckingham Palace Road
London SW1W 0PT

Closing date: 1 February 1999.

The two best designs chosen after the closing date will win a bike!

Answers

See how well you did!

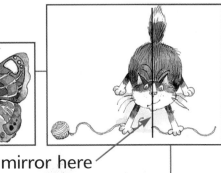

mirror here

Mirror tricks

Mirror Magic
pages 10–11
Secret writing
Rainbows have fun.

Under the Sea
pages 16-17
Starfish spot
There are 15 starfish.
Each one has five legs.
Go dotty
A shark.
Treasure find
Diver 2 leads you
to the treasure.
Matching up the mermaids
Mermaids 3 and 6
are the same.

Body Talk pages 22-23
Body movements

surprised   grumpy   puzzled

Mime game
Three blind mice.

Work out the Wildlife
pages 28-29
1. flamingo, 2. giraffe
3. hedgehog, 4. goldfish
5. frog, 6. ladybird
7. butterfly, 8. zebra.